MYSTIC BRIDGE

Edward Lowbury

MYSTIC BRIDGE

Edward Lowbury

HIPPOPOTAMUS PRESS

ACKNOWLEDGEMENTS are due to the editors of the following: *Acumen, Agenda, Ambit, Encounter, Envoi, London Magazine, The New York Times, Only Poetry, Orbis, Other Poetry, Outposts, Poésie Europe, Poetry Review, The Spectator, Standpoints, Swansea Review, Wave* and to the following anthologies: *A Fifth Poetry Book* (OUP), *Borestone Mountain Poetry Awards 1977, PEN New Poetry, 1977.*

For Shakespeare on his 400th birthday was commissioned by The Globe Playhouse Trust and published in *Poems for Shakespeare (1974); A Triptych for Henry Purcell* was written for the Birmingham Chamber Music Society to be read at its Purcell Tercentenary Concert in 1995.

I am grateful to my wife for valuable suggestions and help.

We thank Colin Scott-Sutherland for permission to use the picture by his father as the cover illustration

First published 1997 by
HIPPOPOTAMUS PRESS
22, Whitewell Road, Frome, Somerset.

© Edward Lowbury 1997

A CIP Record for this book is available from the
British Library Cataloguing in Publication Data Office

ISBN 0 904179 61 3

*Ten copies only have been numbered and signed
by the author*

Cover illustration: water colour by Edwin Scott Sutherland

Printed in Great Britain by
Latimer Trend & Company Ltd, Plymouth, Devon

For

John Press

CONTENTS

I

II

I

THREE PHILOSOPHERS
(For Roy Lewis)

Afternoon tea: our guests, two
Professors of philosophy,
John Scott and Leonard Russell,
Explore the everlasting
Enigmas of our language,
Float some new definitions.

In a rare moment of silence
Ruth, our four-year-old, shouts,
"Daddy, what are things for?"
"Ask Uncle John, ask Leonard,"
I chuckle, remembering
One poet's definition
Of a four-year-old: "Thou best
Philosopher, thou eye
Among the blind…"

        But our
Visiting professors, John
Scott and Leonard Russell,
Smile silently at us
And at each other, knowing
The best answer to a question
May be another question
Or, failing that, just silence.

A TOUCH OF THE SUN

A touch of jaundice: dry leaves
Brush my forehead as they float
Down to the wet pavement,
Reminding me of harder times:
September thirty-nine
Mocking us with silent beauty
Soon to be snatched back;
And then the red sky falling,
Blockbusters, Spitfires
Shooting their hearts out,
Death dropped from a burning zenith:
Sick dreams from which
I staggered, all clear, at dawn
To the chord of thanksgiving;
Lit up and still alive
I stumbled through an open wall
Into the apparition
Of London, its dust in the air;
Down streets of broken homes,
A few left standing,
Eviscerated; a naked
Bath, a bed, a table were
Revealed at the stripped edge
Of an upper room, its flowered paper
Flapping in the breeze...

But suddenly the lid
Blows off: fresh light
Skims the shining pavement
And brings me to my senses:
It's nineteen eighty-nine
And I'm still here... A leaf
Shot through with yellow light
Drifts down across my path,
Frisks me. It's an autumn
I dared not hope to see;

And here, beside the pavement,
Is a playing field, with rituals
Of a new autumn term—
Mock battle, the scrum,
The flying tackle, the shouts,
A whiff of cold sweat.
Decades ago I too
Observed those rituals,
A slave to the system,
Hating every moment.

Old soldier, survivor
Of both World Wars,
Secure behind sixty years
From scrum and flying tackle,
From jeers and cold sweat,
Enjoy your liberty—
The sere and yellow leaf!
A touch of jaundice? No—
But a sharp touch of the sun.

SPRING-CLEANING AT EIGHTY

"Thank you for having me," I was taught to say
    To the mothers of my friends
        Before going home after a party:
It's time I started to thank Mother Earth that way!

There's much to be thankful for... our daily bread,
    Friendship and love, good health—
        And freedom not to pretend I believe
That I'll go on living even when I am dead;

And that a magnificent old man with a beard
    Created the expanding
        Universe: it used to be
A capital offence to call such claims absurd,

A sin to tell the truth, virtue to fake
    Conviction, to swear 'I believe':
        A paradox, but perhaps not strange
When the prospect was not hellfire, but the stake!

I'm giving thanks where thanks are due, to the power
    On earth that can, we know,
        Create new life, animal, vegetable,
Human; real, though inscrutable as the hour.

Its name is Life; hatched by the lifeless sun,
    It deserves the hallelujahs,
        Temples, cathedrals, icons
Mankind has raised to the Imagined One.

But that leaves out what staggers me still more:
    The unquestionable Fact
        Of a first cell, of a moment when
That cell divided, two cells, and then four...

Stranger than a virgin birth, something from nothing,
 The Nativity of Life;
  Today it even seems that what
Mother Earth kept dark she now may be unearthing,

The light of DNA: I sing and shout
 My thanks for this revelation,
  Something to know and keep, in place
Of what I merely believed and now cast out.

But wait... What forced that first cell to break free?
 Perhaps I sang too soon...
  Until we trace Time to its birth
God will, it seems, preserve His Mystery.

WALNUT

This walnut casts a subtle spell:
   It's a man's brain in miniature,
   Twin convoluted hemispheres
Protected by a cranial shell;

A mocking imitation, though!
   Quaint Nature's picture of a brain,
   As powerless and senseless as
A pebble, and as cold as snow.

What am I saying?   Senseless? — Yes:
   Shrewd Nature never meant a seed
   To rhyme or think or flex a limb:
That's not its job. But powerless?

My brain, which rhymes and loves and hates,
   Cannot, as this thing can, compose
   A forest tree, — the living green
That every poem celebrates.

VIRTUAL REALITY (For Roland John)

You say you would like to climb K2 or Everest
   Not so much to be there
      As to feel what being there is like;
Then maybe all you need is to make do

With 'virtual reality'; that should keep you safe
   From avalanches, falls
      And frostbite; without leaving
Your chair you'll have the excitements of the climb;

And that goes, too, for piloting Concorde,
   Or riding to the moon
      On a space-ship, or even,
Perhaps, for falling in or out of love...

Yet what makes all the difference between virtual
   And real reality
      Is just the danger and the dread
You think you are spared by 'virtuality';

What virtue lies in virtual love-making?
   What safety lies in knowing
      That you can switch the whole thing off,
The joy—or pain, like a dream from which you are waking?

And what about virtual *un*reality?
   Those space invaders, djinns,
      Ghouls, abominable snowmen,
Satan himself, all flagrantly unreal:

Suppose their unreality 'virtual':
   They are then as real to you
      As tigers, vipers, viruses;
Menacing, though we pretend they are unreal;

A virtual friend breaks through our lines of defence;
  Though it is hard to tell
    What's real from what is virtual,
That difference, friend, makes all the difference!

MIXED-UP

Is it surprising that we are so mixed-up
When God has planted in our species seeds
Of paradox? To begin with, being fathered
Through a duct which serves also for waste-disposal,
A serious joke; and then mothered, born
Through a channel betwixt Scylla and Charybdis,
'*Inter faeces et urinam*'; later to find
The unmentionable act a synonym
For the earthly paradise, through which are born,
With pain, creatures little less than the angels,
(And who has seen an angel?)... What wonder
Our speech reflects all this madcap confusion;
That it bursts through the barriers of correctness,
Spitting the curse which means ' the earthly paradise';
But worse than that, when a brain tries to correct
The body's contradictions, redesigns
Its functions, turning cocks to guns and fires them
At foes, at passers-by, at kith and kin,
And drives a lecherous lout to simulate
The act of love in an orgasm of hate,
Then whips him on to mutilate and kill.

What have the fires of love, of harmony
To do with arson, bombs and conflagrations?
Are Hell's destructive thunderbolts the same
As the creative lightnings Beethoven,
Shakespeare and Michelangelo converted
To immortal artefacts which show us mortals
What angels look like, grant a glimpse of God?
And can those lightnings also be the ecstasy
Of mania, the fiery sword of schizophrenia,
Or the clumsy mixed-up falls of Jack and Jill?

MOTHER'S DAY

Where shall a man whose mother died before
Her son was born, before even *she* was born,
Present his gift of sunflowers? Perhaps
At the gate of a hospital in which that egg
Was plucked from a lifeless foetus, fertilised
And planted like a sunflower seed inside
The body of a woman he calls 'Mother'?
Or should it not be *she*, whose love provided
His wants from the moment of conception, fed,
Sheltered and cherished him, to whom the sunflowers
Should be presented? Surely she is the one
He loves, not a cold anonymous foetus
Which might have been his mother had it lived.

Note: The possibility of using eggs from dead foetuses instead of from
donors has been suggested for the treatment of infertility.

THE TRUE MODERNITY

'Evil, be thou my good,
    Discord my harmony,'
Roars Vitriol; 'I practise
    The true modernity!'

But surely, Vitriol,
    For those you praise there should
Be no such dated ciphers
    As 'harmony' and 'good'?

ECCLESIASTES

'Vanity of vanities',
    The Preacher thundered, 'all
Is vanity; we rise
    That we may blindly fall.'

But taste those words again
    In a more sober mood:
If all good things are vain
    Some vanities are good.

GIFT (For Lionel Pyetan)

Each January a gift—
Oranges from Israel:
A boxful of sunrises
Beaming rays of hope,
Warmth, loving-kindness;
Ascorbic rays lightening
Our daylight through the darkest month.

Friend, you have more sun
In Jaffa than you need,
Won't miss what's in this box;
And yet, what you have sent us
Is a transfusion, lifeblood
To accelerate our movements,
Rectify this anaemia.

In an age of stones and bullets,
In a land where Moses' rules
Give place to Darwin's law,
How can you spare a pint
Of that most precious ichor
For us, whose only grumbles
Are illness and foul weather?

I am eating them, turn this fruit
Into myself... Full of the spell
You cast in sending them,
I have a guilty feeling:
See differently this year
What's left inside that box
Half-full of golden sunsets.

SMALL TIGER (For Ursula Vaughan Williams)

Today's Big Cat is an endangered species—
   The man-eater is being snuffed out by man;
But—fiercely calm, disdainful of man's wishes,
   The Small Tiger is an Olympian,

Burning bright on the hearth, its half-shut eye
   Lucent, compelling us to stroke and feed,
To watch in adoration from on high,
   Serving obediently each purring need.

Poets, composers, painters praise the cat;
   Tom Gray loved Selima, who had a fall
Into a bowl of goldfish, doffed his hat
   To her memory; Tom Eliot loved them all;

And Peter Warlock stopped a bus, jumped off
   To stroke an unknown puss that caught his eye
On a garden fence... What moved those three was Love
   Which moves the sun and stars in the distant sky,

Plus a profound respect, a streak of dread
   On seeing one so small, yet fiercely calm,
Cuddly but taloned, and quite unafraid
   Of the giant whom it beards without a qualm.

And here on earth the little cat survives,
   While Big Cats are wiped out. Moggie will win
Through love-with-a-dash-of-fear, its nine lives
   Preserved by the tiger underneath the skin.

CHICKWEED

Definitive weed, but starriest of flowers,
   I pluck huge armfuls of you from the rosebed,
    Then mutter apologies: I'm half ashamed
Of having scotched your blaze of tiny stars,
Cut short a living galaxy. My peace
   Of mind is oddly jarred; soothing my nerves,
    I say that I have killed the weeds to save
The roses. Now I'm trying to save face…
Soon they will hatch, dog roses, floribunda;
   No doubt I'll sing their praise, as I have done
    Each summer, but this year I will reserve
Some harmony, some living words of wonder
For midget, self-effacing stars of day
Which live, outshining midnight's Milky Way.

SERENADE

At 5 a.m.—a serenade:
   This solo blackbird on the roof
     Puts me to shame, starting his day
While I am staggering back to bed!

He flings his gauntlet of bright song,
   Scaring the wits of smaller fry:
     Shrill soundbites which, for me, spell joy,
Kaleidoscopic shots of Spring.

Not aimed at me, this sniping drives
   Back tits and finches, which fight back
     With their own laser beams of song—
For this is War... or is it Love?

THE UNPROCESSED WORD
(For Malcolm Williamson)

In this age of the word-processor you are sending
   Hand-written letters; friends are glad you do:
Like fingerprints and faces, the handwriting
   Is yours alone: that manuscript is *you*.

Virtual reality of a flawless typescript
   Leaves out essentials—whispers barely heard,
The heartbeats, and what moves between the lines...
   Thank you for giving me your Unprocessed Word.

RECOGNISING THEIR KIND

(1) Beauty and the Beast

Why should a dog, which doesn't see a mirror,
Know that it's not a cat? What urges beasts
And birds to herd and pair with their own kind?
I dream a kind of answer; seem to be
The Beast whom Beauty rescued; when I look
At Beauty, all my features seem to change
Halfway to hers; I have become a mirror
That half-reflects her contours... Yes, but now
I notice, with dismay, her shape has changed
(Through love? Through sympathy?) halfway towards mine.
She recognises the dark prince inside
My tusked and horny carapace, while I,
Perhaps, have sniffed and guessed the animal
Hidden inside the angel that she seemed.

(2) What is Beauty?

What is it that compels me to admire
One face more than the rest, some more than others?
A secret voice whispers the answer: "Genes
In all your cells picture a unique shape,
THE HUMAN FACE, by which a human eye
Will recognise its kin and move towards it;
The faces that you see which most resemble
The genes' picture are by definition
The shapeliest." As a magnet that compels
Anything made of iron to move towards it,
The shapeliest face attracts all human kind,
The scorpion's shape attracts all scorpions—
Even to be swallowed at the nuptial feast...
Such a definition of beauty should reach out
To gravitation, which controls the antics
Of heaven... Dante got it nearly right.

SPEAK, PARROT (For Yann Lovelock)

Language— what do you call it?   A golden chain,
   An Orphic song, the signature
      Of Man, — his knack of making noises
That carry thoughts or news; a joy; a pain;

A bridgehead; maker or breaker of fences...
   Perhaps it would be better
      If language were just verbal music—
The sense indefinite; — then those differences,

The seeds of war, could not exist, for words
   That are meaningless could not
      Be misconstrued; there's no dispute
Between loquacious parrots or minah birds.

From time to time we're taught where we belong
   Through language: the upstart
      Builders of Babel suddenly found
They did not understand their mother tongue,

While a gift of tongues, a flame of understanding
   What once was foreign, fell
      On humble men of praise and wonder
Suddenly aware of the fences they were mending.

And yet our world is just as full of fear,
   As plagued with feud and torture
      As it was before those miracles:
Headstones galore cry, ' Talking brought me here:'

Meaning is irrelevant: even if it's no more
   Than music, the sound
      Your words make might anger
The people and become the seeds of war.

"Speak, Parrot... of franticness and foolishness,"
   Sang Skelton; I add
     An answering voice, "Speak, Man:
Your words are parrot-wisdom, more or less."

TWO TAPE RECORDINGS

(1) Traveller in Time (Remembering Andrew Young)

Longing for a way to put Time into reverse,
   To go—not merely look—back to the past,
You searched inside your skull for the region where,
   We like to suppose, all ages co-exist;

Then stumbled on a way—the tape recording
   Of your own talk, but played back twice as fast,
And what you were saying in the voice of an old man
   Came back in a child's treble and panting haste.

(2) Amour Propre?

Tape your own voice, then play that record back
   At twice the speed: at once the sound will be
A high soprano, female of the species:
   A sex-change not induced by surgery.

Hearing that voice, some prowling male might scent
   A dazzling temptress, strive to track her down...
Even you, in an absent-minded hour, might drop
   That clanger, forgetting the voice was once your own!

EXCLAMATION MARKS

Poco sofferse me cotal Beatrice,
e commincio, raggiandomi d'un riso
tal, che nel foco faria l'uom felice
                    Dante: *Paradiso* VII. 16-18

'Why are your letters full of exclamation marks?'
   She asks me. I reply, ' Perhaps because I find
Surprises all around, and want to share with you
   The excitement; there'd be more full stops if I were
                                        blind!

But that's not all: an exclamation mark is like
   A smile; I try to show you what I'm thinking of
While writing; I reflect, in thought, your smiling face,
   Having seen how that smile could light the fires of love.'

"X"

Two lovers, with bare arms
   About each others' waists,
Under this foliage
   Are shadowy as ghosts;

And yet their arms, which glow
   Behind them, make a sly
Quotation of that stern
   Commandment, 'Multiply.'

ARRESTED INTIMACIES

Though a stranger's, her face,
Admired day by day
As he passed the open door
Near which she sat working,
Always looked back at him
As though in expectation;
Those moments were his life—
Arrested intimacies,
Their lightning brevity
The concentrate of hours.
Almost as intense, the moment
When a nameless girl
Sat on an airport bench
Beside him, sending shock
Waves along the shared plank,
Proximity a challenge,
Almost an intimacy.

'So little,' he reflected,
'Can generate so much.'
What super-voltage, then,
Should pass between those two
Sitting in married silence
On the opposite bench? They stare
Or scowl in vacancy,
And seem to be expecting
Some power to cut the bonds
That shackle them together...
Yet they too, perhaps,
Long ago, in a brief
Storm of thirst, lived
Only to win the bonds
Which now they yearn to cut.

A SMILE

Passing the place where lovers part,
I catch the remnant of a smile
Full in the face; not meant for me;
Like catching cold, an influence
So strong, it dominates the day;
A germ to which my cells won't learn
Immunity.

Not meant for me, that smile dropped
Like a bud from a bouquet.
I pick it up and hold it,
Can't set it free, can't free myself;
The sudden glow, the light
Of those translated features
Dictate their own reflection.

So I reflect, become a mirror,
Camera to proclaim, record
This rainbow, the smile I saw
On a girl's face—until my own
Leers back, reflected from a window,
And in a flash my smile becomes
A loud guffaw.

UNANSWERED LETTERS

Suddenly the negative becomes positive.
My letters have dropped dead—
No answers from a loved one abroad,
From a friend who promised help,
From the old lady who said 'Do write,
I am lonely.'
Not like messages dispatched in bottles
Or sent up on toy balloons
Which had no destination,
These reached theirs, and reaped
The brush-off, or the kiss of death.

And now, like a print raised
From an indecipherable film,
A sort of answer hits me—
But by the same flash I see
In a dark corner of my room
Those letters, those entreaties
Which I have left unanswered,
Delaying week by week;
Perplexed by indecision; at last
Shutting my senses to their cry
And thinking that, with silence
And slow time, they too
Would spring a positive
And answer themselves.

PHYSICS OF LOVE

This optional extra light
   Should pacify the earth
And be reflected back
   On those who gave it birth;

But some on whom it smiles
   Transform the energy
To grinding hate—or cast
   Shadows of apathy.

BLACK LIGHT

Eyebeams—the black light
That shines out from the heart of the eye—
Can't move a mote of dust
But strike down the hard-headed:
For those who put up shutters
Against love, this laser
Breaks through and lays them low;
And those who look with hate
On all that stand in their way
Blacken those at whom they stare.
Having discovered both
Effects of that black light,
Shield your eyes and think twice
Before you use the same weapon.

A POSTHUMOUS INTIMACY

That ring you lost—black opal (was it?) set
In diamonds, the legacy of an aunt
You hardly knew: it's irreplaceable.
Not much to look at when compared with things
You are offered free—clouds, hills, fire,
Forests, faces—and not often looked at,
Though valued at a thousand pounds, they say.

By contrast, here are things disposable,
Things neat and useful, to be thrown away
Once used—a pot, a wrapper, a syringe;
And at my feet, walked over, there are stones
To rival opals; they are the ones for me,
All mine for nothing, priceless in a sense,
Commodities that money cannot buy.

They are like us; like them we are disposable,
Unmarketable, quickly replaced when dead.
Yet one or two, our kin, are like the opal;
Indeed, still dearer, priceless in a sense
And irreplaceable; even that aunt
You hardly knew struck up a posthumous
Intimacy, now lost with the ring she left you.

SANDWRITING

Scrawled in the wet sand
At low tide: 'STEVE LOVES
HILARY FOREVER.'
Like an epitaph for a grave
Still to be dug, the message
Shares with love itself
A disbelief in Time.

Time doesn't count for much
With Steve's brow unwrinkled
And Hilary's cheek porcelain;
'Forever' means a permanent 'Now';
The clock repeats itself
From day to day, and smiles
In friendly collusion.

But this wet sand is covered
With tiny wrinkles; rising
Water covers dreams, castles;
And a now unsmiling clock
Has something new to say:
"Forever" means "Until
The next high tide."

A THOUGHT FOR FEMINISTS

'Madam Chairperson' or, more bluntly , 'Chair',
   Why have you banned the gentle suffix, 'man'?
'Man' is a pun, means 'male' but also 'human',
   So is it logical to impose that ban?

And what is 'woman'? Ask the O.E.D.
   It tells you 'wife-man'. So, fret as you may,
There's no escaping from it; you must be
   What you have always been, one kind of 'man'!

VIVE LA DIFFÉRENCE

" 'Roes' equals 'Rose'; examine that equation.
   Can you conceive two things more different
Yet more alike?" he asked—an examination
   Poser! I saw exactly what he meant,

That when you hear them spoken, the two words
   Are indistinguishable, and that they both
Mean organs of reproduction. Afterwards
   I imagined myself swearing a solemn oath:

"Rose is a rose is a rose!" Rose is a name
   By which we know a plant, a girl, a flower;
With 'roes' the picture is not quite the same;
   Their provenance is fishy, and no power

On earth can change the way these herring roes
By any other name might strike your nose!

MORGAN: A Sestina

They seemed a perfect match: he strong, humane,
Articulate; she seductive, gentle, frank;
Both keen to praise, unwilling to condemn;
Seemingly much in love. I wondered why
At forty Morgan was a curate still;
Too unambitious, maybe, or too kind?

At twenty I was brash and less than kind
To some who failed. My words were inhumane
When France let Hitler in: "You see, they're still
The same," I said, "these friends, so proud, so frank;
They've let us down!" And Morgan whispered "Why?"—
Then grabbed my arm and cried, "Never condemn."

His words kept haunting me, "Never condemn."
Brooding on them, I must have grown more kind
Through years when I'd lost sight of him. But why
Was Morgan kinder to those less humane
Than to himself? — The newspapers were frank:
"He killed himself while mad, a curate still."

"He's cured at last," I sighed,"his heart is still:
'Age cannot weary him, nor the years condemn'—
Sop for the fallen, Binyon's; if not frank,
At least well-meant"…Morgan had been too kind
To a choirgirl, she too human, too humane;
So they were caught in bed together. — "Why?"

Exploded his cold, loveless wife: and "Why?"
She cried again, now widowed. She was still
Seductive, calm, but had she been humane
To Morgan? When in bed, did she condemn
His ardour, or his failure? Was it kind
To leak his earlier lapses? Was it frank?

I'll answer that with "No, it was not frank
For her to whisper, 'He's unfaithful' ." Why?
Because she hid stains of another kind.
She talked, and he remained a curate still...
But now I catch his words, "Never condemn!"
The words live on, articulate, humane.

Dear Morgan, you were frank when I was still
Censorious; "Why?" you asked. "Never condemn,"
You preached—too kind to live, and too humane.

MISMATCH

Woman excites his instinct to protect;
    he sees her as a grown-up child,
her voice unbroken, still a piping treble,
    her skin smooth as it was when five years old.

And she resents his arrogance: 'Why should
    he think himself more competent?
Because his voice is deep, his chin bearded?
    A patronising assumption—kindly meant!'

The Guardians sigh: 'For "instinct to protect"
    read "instinct to possess";'
but even his child is not his property,
    and his wife is *more* competent, not less!

The Guardians shake their heads: 'God made the sexes
    different, complementary;
often that works... But War, not Love, breaks out
    when one is what the other yearns to be.'

A TRIPTYCH FOR HENRY PURCELL AT THE TERCENTENARY OF HIS DEATH

I

John Blow, Master of Music to the King,
   Saw the divine spark
      In one young pupil, made him take
His own place, to play, compose and sing.

Singing before King Charles seemed like a rehearsal
   For the heavenly choir... John boasted,
      After his pupil's death, that he
Had once been teacher of the famous Henry Purcell.

II

Bright diamond in a bright
musical constellation,
I'm listening tonight

to your starbeams' commotion
filling a heaven inside my head.
You're a godsend to our nation

which is not overfed
with its own music. You
(though at forty you were dead)

left us a dazzling view
in a dark part of the sky:
shapes fanciful yet true.

Why did you have to die,
being an immortal? — Song,
sonata, fantasy,

opera, anthem, tongue-
in-cheek inventions dropped
effortless from your young

clairvoyance... then it stopped.
Three centuries on, they're heard,
those strains time can't corrupt,

notes fancy-free as a bird
singing: these we inherit.
So I sing (with Hopkins' word

to proclaim your order of merit)
this celebratory morsel
for 'so arch-especial a spirit

as heaves in Henry Purcell.'

III

Could he foresee how brief would be his time?
   Outpacing Death, he raced
      Ahead, in league with rhymers, and
With one, John Dryden, who was a prince of rhyme.

Too early, though, it came, the harsh reversal
   Of fortune, when Death
      Caught up with him, — but not with
My theme and variations, *Henry Purcell.*

FOR SHAKESPEARE,
on his 400th birthday

The isle is full of noises,
Sounds and sweet airs that give delight,
and hurt not. (The Tempest)

This long retarded Spring
With force of a coiled wire
Bursts out from everything:

From wood, a green fire—
Small sparks at first, but then
A blaze; the phoenix choir

Of birds, after ten
Months' abstinence, complete
And flawless. Like men

Starved, then offered meat,
We burst out of our cells
To find the sun's heat;

And savour something else,
Quite new, though heard before—
A ringing of our bells

And knockings at the door
When neighbours bring hot news
From haunted Elsinore,

Or argue whom they'd choose
To govern the domain
Of mad King Lear; then lose

Our bearings and remain
With magus Prospero—
The day come round again

When, having tricked the foe,
He found his blest isle
Four centuries ago,

And blazed here for a while.

THE POET

The paper caught fire under his pen;
For a moment earth and sky were ablaze
And the light came from the paper.
But it burned; the sheet turned to ashes,
The fire went out.
And now when someone asks him
For a scrap of paper, he searches

Through pockets, drawers, and finds them empty.

PORTRAIT BY CHANCE

For a moment this excellent likeness
    Of your profile takes shape
In a silver cloud. Almost at once
    It changes: the lips gape,
The nose fragments, the profile
    Becomes your caricature,
And then, by stages, a bull
    A cat, a dinosaur...

Pure chance? Then Chance deserves
    Praise for having drawn
Your portrait as well as Rembrandt
    Might have done it by design:
For having drawn the original
    As well; — for letting me discover
Chance can perform the same

    Miracle twice over.

TWO ARTISTS

(1)

"Your drawing has the mark of permanence;
    Stop now! An extra line will ruin it.
You can't improve a thing beyond perfection."
    Everyone told him that.

But he forged on, perversely crowding out
    The living family he'd created; filled
Every unoccupied space with lines and figures,
    Turning the purest gold

Back to base metal... With a mocking laugh
    He answered us: "I imitate my teacher;
He is not Cézanne, Rembrandt or Michelangelo,
    But an earlier Creator

Who carried on after the Seventh Day
    And went on adding lines to faces, figures
To landscapes, filling every empty space
    With life. His art beggars

Description; by an inverted alchemy
    He turns base gold to iron, allowing none
But the fittest to survive—and even they
    Are here for a day, then gone."

(2) (For William Gear)

On a beach where topless beauties draw the eye
    Sits Bill, Master of abstract form, drawing
A human shape he has found on the rock face,
    Makes that his model; he knows what he is doing,

50

Copying God's own portrait of His own
    Creative masterpiece; done to perfection
And permanent as rock: here is the gift
    Bill craves —substance wedded to abstraction.

PORTRAIT OF TIME

The digital clock-face lacks a pulse, a heart
    Like those which tick inside
Clocks with a human countenance, Big Ben,
    Grandfather's turnip, or this watch—
My thirteenth birthday present. Two black hands,
    The features of that face, strike patterns
That spark so many different sorts of feeling
    At different times of day or night;
Vigour or drowsiness at twelve; excitement
    Or tedium at nine; comfort
At half-past four... an artist's view of Time
    Pulsating, brimful of life—
Face with a heart. But the artist who paints Time
    As a digital face would miss all that,—
Would picture Man as a computer print-out
    And the clock as a death-mask of Time.

CHILDREN AT A CONCERT

They are chattering all at once
    Before it starts, like starlings—
        A sibilant chance chorus
Of jibes, hoots, puns:
A fluttering counterpoint
    Of expectation spilling over
        Into the old folks' ears
With timeless merriment:
The great discoveries—
    Beethoven's Fifth, Messiah,
        The Magic Flute — the ground
We stand on: all these
For them are still to come; for us
    The magic starts to fade:
        We shop around for fresh
Measures to spring surprise,
Search for untrodden ground:
    And here is something fresh,
        This chattering madrigal
Of bright unhackneyed sound.

CELLO FANTASY (For an unborn grandchild)

'... trailing clouds of glory do we come'
Wordsworth

Your foetal ears
Pick up a message from the outer world—
An inkling of Time, when
Your mother's cello utters
Apocalyptic notes, the opening
Of a Beethoven sonata
A mere hand-span away.

Through life that phrase may haunt you
As a rainbow memory of the timeless home,
The eternity from which you fell,
Trailing clouds of glory.

No wonder the music a soul brings down to earth
From heaven should draw him back
To that timeless inner world,
Even as the analyst's fantasy, a wish
To return to the womb—
Where he first heard a music breaking in
From the outer world of Time.

COMPOSER'S DREAM
(For John Joubert who had the dream)

Why should a dream corrupt the following day?
This one, perhaps, had something more to say;
Sinister as an escape of nuclear waste
It choked my thoughts and left a bitter taste.

On the stone pavement of the music school
Appeared a gap, through which I saw a pool
Of bubbling, viscous water. Someone said
'Look—the primordial slime!' Thrilled, but afraid
At being let into the secret of creation—
Or at least, of a spontaneous generation—
I watched the slime yield up a human shape
Which rose to the gap as if struggling to escape..
I dragged it out—a corpse; then many more
Followed the first, lay scattered on the floor.

Waking from a dream much more intense than day
I wondered, what was it all trying to say?
Those stillborn creatures cast up in the home
Of music, were they embodiments of some
Disaster—of the composer's hidden fears,
Dead compositions, or dead listeners?

MUSIC OF THE SPHERES

Waking at 3 a.m. when there's no traffic,
    When silence should be undisturbed, I hear
This ringing in my ears, like a seraphic
    Choir in the upper register. Sudden fear:
What might it mean? Deafness? Perhaps a stroke?
    Sudden death? I stop my ears, but still
    That whistling choir goes on, against my will:
Try to ignore it, but—without fire, no smoke...

I open the window and look out; not deaf,
    Thank goodness! I can hear the leaves rustle,
And a distant hum scored in the bass clef—
    Night shift at the works; and still that whistle,
High up: seeing Cassiopeia, I fancy
    That is her voice, a Music of the Spheres
    Too high-pitched, too ethereal for most ears;
A voice from outer space, erratic, chancy.

Of course, the ethereal choir is in my head;
    But Cassiopeia up there, Queen of the Night,
Might by this time, for all I know, be dead—
    It is so long since those pinpricks of light
That stir me here blazed out from separate stars;
    They were no constellation till they fell—
    Five seraphs tickling each optic cell
To sing behind my cranial prison bars.

AT KIRKSTALL ABBEY
(For Kathleen)

More beautiful, perhaps, in ruins than
    It seemed in life, this tattered masonry—
      The windows baring one sky to another,
      Transmitting gales or fair weather—
    Is only part of what I see:
The mind's eye fills the gap as best it can.

It's like a skull which, if you look at it
    Not as a symbol of death, but as a thing,
      May have more beauty than the face it wore,
      Relieved of worries, plagued no more
    By sagging flesh; in life, perhaps, a king
Or zombie? — now it matters not one bit.

A GARDEN (For Vivian and Patsy Meynell)

When I was young this garden had no trees,
   No shelter from the August sun;
      But it could answer back
        With its own floral blaze,
        And on most days
      I could put up with such a lack.
   In the middle of the lawn there stood
A haggard statue with a hole in its head
     Called 'John the Baptist';
       From its open mouth
     And empty eyes came light
That seemed to have some meaning,
      Hints of a startling and unfathomed truth.

But now, forty years on,
   Trees that were seedlings then—
      Sycamore, oak and black-leaved beech—
      Have grown to giant size and reach
   Up to the roof, across the lawn,
      Casting cold shadow, leaving hardly
      A loophole for the sun;
The flowers are scanty, seeming doubtful of their role.
     From the Baptist's open mouth and eyes
      There flows no light—
The eyes are blank, the mouth is a black hole.

CREATING LIGHT

A nine-year-old in bed
With magic—a bull's eye torch,
His birthday present, — feels like
The Creator as he makes light
In the darkness. How easy:
Like saying 'Let there be Light!'
Indeed, searching the ceiling
With a focused beam, he feels
He is creating more
Than light; chairs, shoes,
Shelves suddenly spring
From nothing into sharp focus.
'Let there be Light,' he murmurs,
Knowing the first thing
Created, after heaven and earth,
Was light; but could that be?
The Mouth which gave the order
Created words first,
And so — 'Let there be Sound.'
He mutters, half asleep...

But then his imp sister
In the other bed wakes up
And shouts, 'What's that you're doing?'
And the brother, scenting mischief,
Cries out 'Look up, look up!
There's a spider on the ceiling;
Do you see? It's growing bigger.'

The wide open hand
Over the open torch
Squirms and wriggles, casts
A frightening black shadow;
And as it looms closer
To the torch, the shadow swells,
Engulfs the whole room...

The baby sister screams,
And the wicked brother chuckles;
'He'll eat us all up.'
And then to himself, darkly,
'I say "Let there be Darkness." '

III

GAIA A Letter to James Lovelock

Dear James,
                    Reading the *Gaia* someone gave me
At Christmas, I can hear each word as though
It were your voice thinking aloud, serious,
Gently sardonic, whimsical, tentative
But quite sure of itself. Suddenly
I am charmed back to the Common Cold Unit
In Salisbury where, forty years ago,
We hatched some quaint ideas: 'Sneeze-watching'
At lectures and in trains, to see how often
Students, passengers blew—or picked— their noses;
Tracking a germ's route from soul to soul
In a game of cards, with fluorescent tracers;
Counting the germs in patients' handkerchiefs…
The wildest hunches often seemed the best;
Many took flight, a few came home to roost.

In your new book you've hatched a high-flier,
A spaceborne, wingless one—the Earth
Revealed as an animal on which we live
Much as the staphylococci live on us.
You call the creature Gaia, Homer's name
For Mother Earth. Your theme rings true,
Strikes a responsive chord, a shuddering memory
Of a black swarm, a river of soldier ants
Somewhere in Africa—pitiless millions
Marching to slaughter termites—or some camper
Caught sleeping in their path: one ravenous ant,
An outrider, dug ferocious teeth
Into my ankle when I passed. I saw,
As a revelation, that a single ant
Was nothing more than a component cell,
An organ of that animal—the swarm.
Like a voracious leucocyte or a mouth
It had no separate life. Next I recall
A westward flight of geese that suddenly

Switched northward: a mute word of command
Controlled the gaggle; a message from a brain
To its obedient limbs, each bird no more
Than a component cell or organ of
That body of geese. Likewise, the colonies
Of staphylococci growing in my lab
On culture media seemed like organisms,
More than the sum of their component cells,
That little extra linkage giving them
What makes an individual. Like the geese,
These colonies would, for no apparent reason,
Change course at times, all suddenly resistant
To our favourite antibiotic, able now
To infect without restraint.

                 Looking from space
Into the blue, veiled, bloodshot globe, your eye
Recognises its Doppelgänger. "The planet
Is alive!" you sing; and then, laying aside
Your bardic robe, you change roles, put on
Your lab-coat and thinking-cap, argue
The case: "Gaia lives because her climate
Is full of oxygen, which would be scarce
On a dead planet; look at Venus, Mars,
The Moon—all dead. Gaia's alive because
Her molecules are kept exactly right
For life on Earth, any excess or shortage
At once corrected by a power like that
Which rules our heartbeat and controls the weight
Of salt and cells and sugar in our blood,
A power we call *homeostasis*."

                     True,
But surely there's another power, no less
Definitive, the sign-manual of life,
Multiplication: I can see no hint

64

That Gaia, faithful spouse of Uranus,
Our Father Sky, has offspring—except us
(The fruit of human parents) and, maybe,
The stillborn Moon, and that is just as well:
Imagine a nursery of rumbustuous planets
Bursting with life and lusting to take over
Their Mother Earth—the SF writer's dream:
We should have star-wars in deadly earnest
And space-invaders landing every day...
Some funny things go on in outer space—
Black holes that swallow light, mad stars that spin
Like tops; but a more crazy joke would be
Planets dividing like bacteria
Or having sex and giving birth, like plants
And animals.

        I seem to hear you murmur
"Why assume that a celestial living body
Must ape the rules that govern animals
And plants, bacteria and lesser fry?
The rules for microbes are quite different
From those that you and I, that animals
And plants, the greater fry, observe"—But now
You beg the question. "What is life?" you ask,
And have your foregone answer: "It is something
I chose to label 'life' "—but that's a word
Riddled with metaphor; we say a picture
Is 'full of life'—in other words 'alive':
By the same verbal token, a dead rat
May be 'alive with maggots', or a scalp
'Alive with nits'. And some go further still,
Declare their 'Amstrad' is alive, endowed
With a divine intelligence; but a computer
Will do no more than what's built into it
By the designer, who has no idea

How to build consciousness into his toy
As the great Designer built it into us:
We, at least, are conscious, and that's why I can't
Believe we are merely cells of Mother Earth;
We are more like maggots in that lifeless rat.
"Hold on!" (your voice again); "how do you know
The white cells in your blood, which gorge themselves
On raiding microbes, are not cognisant
Of what they are doing, or even that the microbes
Which race across the microscopic field
Are not switched on and relishing their powers?
Gaia's awareness may be something more
Than the sum of all that's going on in all
The sentient creatures on her skin; like your
Dumb leucocytes and microbes she won't tell
What's on her mind; but whether conscious or
Unconscious, microbes, white cells—they're alive,
And so is Gaia. Take a longer look
From outer space (here is a colour print):
Perhaps you'll see it then."

                          Distance, which lends
Enchantment, lets me see the whole round Earth
Which I can never see while I am on it.
Seeing in the dark, seeing through a glass darkly
Lets me pick up those extra frequencies
I miss by daylight,—intimations
Of something far more deeply interfused;
"The Earth revealed in all its shining beauty
Against the deep darkness of space"—your words
(Not words I'm putting in your mouth!) are poetry,
And the emotional fusion—old belief
Plus modern knowledge—generates the awe
Which fathered gods. 'Beauty is truth', you quote,
'Truth Beauty—that is all ye know...and all
Ye need to know'; and now, your own words

On our life-recognising animal instinct—
"What need is there to define what's obvious?"
By-passing vision, we can sense what can't
Be seen, pick up those extra frequencies.
When I stand back from the Earth, as from a picture,
I sense that it's alive—and beautiful;
But standing further back in outer space
I see it shrink to the magnitude of a star,
A point of light, in the company of galaxies,
Quasars, God-in-the Highest, God diffused
Through the whole universe, much as I see
That life, God's microcosm, is diffused
Through Mother Earth.)

            So, James, I'm not surprised,
Still less aghast, that you, the scientist
I envied, who knew Nature to the core
When my career of science was in its nonage,
Are invited to give sermons in cathedrals,
But get rejection slips from *Science*, *Nature*,
The Establishment; our Science Inquisitors
Are hot on heresy, won't pull down the wall
That separates the Two Cultures; won't forgive you
For managing to climb over it one night,
Framing untestable hypotheses,
Even committing the pathetic fallacy
That's banned on both sides of the wall, the notion
That Nature might have feelings, purposes:
Who knows—perhaps new harmony will spring
From that accord? You are in good company:
Though he recanted when confronted by
The Inquisiton, Galileo whispered
"And yet it moves", the Earth we now can see
Moving, revolving "in all its shining beauty";
It moves us too in a language we must drop

When we climb over the estranging Wall,
Reverting to the language which allows
No double meanings, magic, overtones.

One of our quaint ideas in Salisbury—
Yours, I believe—was to collaborate
In a book called *Fabulous Plants*; I even started
Writing my bit, about the Family Tree.
It came to nothing; but today I feel
That I'm once more collaborating with you,
Sending this letter, a 'chorus' to your song
In celebration of our fabulous planet,
And cheers,
          From your old colleague,

                    Edward Lowbury

IV

VISION

'Vision', we said, hearing how things turned out
    Just as the sage predicted; 'no mere guess:
He could see through appearances and probe
    Deep to those roots from which our future springs.'

'I had a vision,' he said; 'an angel stood
    Before me in a blaze of light; a mouth
Close to my face breathed in my ear, whispered
    "The New Jerusalem"—and I woke up.'

But one, stripped of half an eye's vision,
    Says 'Lord, let me keep what's left, to enjoy
The light of common day; spare my first sight,
    And you can keep foresight and second sight.'

SIGHT-BOUND SOUNDBITE

Defective eyesight may bring dividends
of vision which make up,
in part, for what is lost; today, for example,
I kneeled down to pick up from the floor
a scrap of paper—which turned out to be
a patch of sunlight: like a precious ichor
it bathed the hand which tried to lift it up...
I laughed, and saw myself the conjuror's dupe,
being for seven seconds
about to seize an intrusive sunbeam
and throw the thing into the waste-paper basket.

71

SPECTRE OF A ROSE

Nature abhors a vacuum, fills the islands
   Of blindness in this eye
      With pictures, as she fills with sounds
Others can't hear a deaf man's actual silence.

Sometimes I half-see, above my field
   Of vision, a china plate,
      Worcester or Delft; it vanishes
If I try to see it but if, instead, I shield

My eyes or gaze ahead, the phantom fades
   Gradually; later
      It's there again above the page
I'm reading, blue-and-white, or subtler shades.

Today, a terrier is what I half-see—
   Frisking along the pavement
      Ahead of my right foot; I know
It isn't there, but automatically

Mutter 'I'm sorry' when my shoe comes close
   To kicking the apparition...
      Then a gentler phantom takes
The terrier's place — the spectre of a rose.

LOOKING FOR SOMETHING?

Always puzzled, the man I keep seeing
Who charges down the road, stops, turns,
Runs back, stoops to pick up something,
Throws it down, turns again, stoops,
Picks up something, throws it down, runs...

Always alone, he looks as much lost
As what he is looking for; will stop to think
While crossing a road of screaming brakes. A ghost,
He scares off neighbours who might help. Louts
Laugh at the man, shout "Look, the missing link!"

More puzzled than upset, he never speaks
To passers-by, never complains; but sometimes
Growls at baiting boys, spits, shakes
A helpless fist, and then goes on scanning
Gutters, pavements, other people's homes.

I'd like to help—but has he really lost
Anything? When I catch his eye, a look
So vacuous meets mine, I see, at last,
He is seeking something he has never had
And has no clue what it is, or what it's like.

VICTOR

At night his shouts, 'Nurse! Nurse!'
Wake the ward; the nurse comes running—
As much to relieve the stunned nerves
Of the other madly-wakened patients,
As to shift Victor's paralysed limbs an inch or two:
No matter what she does for his comfort,
He starts again as soon as the nurse goes,
At the top of his voice which, by day
Is barely audible—but which
When he was Company Commander on the beaches
Of Normandy, gave the troops
A common thought, a confidence to quench
The paralysis of fear. That voice
Comes back at night now...

Suddenly I remember how, at four, I feared
The night, when even my parents' lights
And voices were switched off
And Night took over—not just lack
Of light, but a gigantic carrion crow,
All-seeing where I was blind,
Driving its wicked ones—the Demon King
With all his goblins, Willie Winkie, the Witch
Of the stone boat, to fly around
Above the wind-blown garden trees:
Powers against which my omnipotent father
Was powerless...
                    Are these the powers that rack
The paralysed mind and body of dazed Victor?
When he wakes up he sees the Carrion Crow
But also—a handsbreadth away—the vaster Darkness
Into which, by a fluke, he didn't fall
When the stroke felled him. In the darkness
He can't see any more than he could see
What lay ahead when, on the beaches,
Above the guns and screaming Stukas,

His voice rang out, 'Follow me!'
Confident, quenching the paralysis of fear,
It rings out again, with pointless power
Against the enemies who are truly friends.

MURDER

Her labours at an end, she barely heard
   'Your baby was born dead... but deformed,'
     The doctor's words: said nothing; perhaps thought,
Through tears, 'God's mercy: think what I've been spared.'

But he had lied; his message should have been
   'Your baby is deformed; he need not live;'
     And she would have cried, madly, 'Spare the child!
Letting him die would be a deadly sin.'

LIFE INSURANCE

A modest premium sets you free
From care: 'LET US INSURE YOUR LIFE',
Screams the blurb—a happy thought,
An instant immortality!

Who would not gladly pay much more
To be assured he will survive
Old age (the illness no one dodges),
Or a thermonuclear war?

But think again: The Tree of Life
They show you has strange foliage—
Not leaves, but bank notes trained to drop,
Like fireballs, on your desolate wife.

TWO SUICIDES

(1) *The Leader*

'He was responsible,' the media screamed;
'Look, he has killed himself, he must have
    known
Something was wrong—it's almost a confession.'
His followers held their peace. He was alone.
He was the Boss: that meant he was to blame
Even if others erred, and so he fell,
Faultless, save for an overplus of conscience
Which screamed inside him, 'Be responsible.'

(2) *The Priest*

Why did we not guess?
When he drank himself blind he was erasing
A world-picture which excluded him;
When he, barely a swimmer, kept on
    plunging
From the top diving board, he half-hoped
There would be no water to receive him:
And when his parishioners plotted secretly
To remove the sick incumbent from his
    living
He was doing his best to remove himself
And succeeded, eventually, with coal gas.

VARIATION ON A THEME OF SIDNEY

"My true love hath my heart and I have his
By just exchange, one for the other given."
(Sir Philip Sidney; *Arcadia.*)

A perfect stranger has your heart;
    The core of you is now in him,
An indispensable spare part—
    Without it he'd be dead. That whim

Which made you plunge into the abyss,
    Like an impersonal act of love
Was, for the stranger, a sharp kiss
    Of life, a lightning from above

That rescued him. Though you are dead
    Your heart lives on, still warm and kind:
It's his heart now... Propped up in bed
    He thanks you; though still, to his mind,

A stranger, you're no longer strange;
That graft's no theft, but just exchange!

A PIG'S HEART

To eat wild goat, chamois or pygarg,
    That is allowed, but 'swine thou shalt not eat,
Because its hoof is cloven...' You've obeyed
    That rule, but suddenly face defeat:

Your heart has broken down; the doctors say
    'There is one remedy, to have a transplant—
A pig's heart, now that we have found a way
    To ensure it will be permanent.'

You turn this over in your mind: to be
    Or not to be? To choose a pig's life—
The core of you pure pig, or to choose death?
    I think you'll choose the healing knife.

And that's good sense,—gives you an extra reason
    For keeping the Mosaic ritual
Never to swallow pork or ham or bacon:
    You might be branded cannibal!

For what it says in Deuteronomy
    Is 'Thou shalt neither eat nor touch dead swine;'
But that swine's heart sewn into you would be
    As much alive as yours or mine.

DONOR FACE

(A plastic surgeon, Mr Roy Sanders, is researching
the possibility of face transplants for patients with
severe facial burns)

It fits you like a glove,
   This face of an unknown
Bystander that I've grafted
   On the embers of your own.

He fell to a stray bullet,
   But lives again on you,
Rescued, reincarnated
   By surgery, as—who?

I'd like to think the brain cells
   Inside you were the star
Of your identity,—but no:
   Your face is who you are.

TWO OPERATIONS UNDER LOCAL ANAESTHETIC

(For John Alexander-Williams)

I

In a valium trance, watching
The surgeon probe, dissect,
I am suddenly half-aware
Who is the patient; see
My Doppelgänger, the reflection
In a theatre lamp above me,
His wound just where mine is,—
A sympathetic ghost;
A saint of sorts, showing
Mysterious stigmata.

But as I watch, entranced,
The reflection seems to grow
Sharper, and the reflected
Wound deeper than mine;
An embodiment of pain;
While I, floating painless
And disembodied, find
The tables turned, become
The Doppelgänger, show
Mysterious stigmata.

II

This hand anaesthetised,
Seems now to have become
The hand of a cold stranger;
By accident it brushes
My other hand, which shrinks
Away; then—recalling
How once, as though by accident,
A girl's hand brushed mine,
Sparking delight—it reaches out
For the mysterious stranger.

With eyes shut I seem
To recognise that presence;
But while sensation seeps
Back to the dormant nerves,
The two hands become
Like fingers of a single hand,
Again so much at one.
They touch without a trace
Of shrinking irritation
Or sensual delight.

THE BOOK

A hollow book, Shaw's *Plays Pleasant*,
  The pages excavated
    To make an oblong cavity
For cigarettes, was someone's joke-present

One Christmas. That was before we knew about
  Lung cancer sparked by fags;
    Even so, I rampaged against
The headless donor, calling him a lout

For raping *Candida,* savaging *The Man*
  Of Destiny... But progress
    Lopes on unchecked: only today
The Book, the Bible of the World, began

This new career:— its hollow centre packed
  With dynamite, it burst
    In the face of a good man, who died
Unaware that a Bible sparked the unholy act.

HOW LONG IS A DAY?
(For John Joubert)

A day is a long time
   For a child of two or three;
From breakfast-time to lunch
   Is an eternity.

At six, he still may find
   The day too long—a hell
Of boredom through which
   He waits for the school bell;

At home, though, he gets lost
   In a paradise of play:
A day is then more like
   A season than a day.

His hill-climbing elders
   Curse time, but have no power
To slow it down: for them
   A day is more like an hour,

Until—at sixty, say—
   They see, without pain,
Each hour a greater fraction
   Of the years that still remain;

Eternity drifts back;
   The hills stop calling 'Climb!'
And once again, in a sense,
   A day is a long time.

PASSENGERS

They used to call us passengers
    On the Cheltenham Flyer, the Royal Scot:
That put the emphasis on *us*,
    On our departures, arrivals.
The echoes were harmonious.

Now we are labelled 'customers':
    The emphasis is on our *fare*—
On what they take, on what we pay.
    There are no echoes; profitless,
The Flyer's name has flown away.

AFTER PLATO

'Amicus Plato, sed magis amica veritas': after Aristotle

Cowardly men, said Plato, are reincarnated as women,
  Fools as fishes or reptiles. How could the wisest of men
Utter such fatuous nonsense! — or is it we who are crazy,
  Missing some devilish irony or a few slips of the pen?

Soul of man is immortal, he tells us; but what is the point of
  That, if not even a dim recollection persists, in the mind,
From its last innings? Plato could lie, being mainly an artist
  Painting a scene to which every 'immortal' is equally
                                    blind.

LIES

Nature, you say, can't lie:
Why then should she pretend
An orchid is a bee—
Or that my feet lifting
The bedclothes are mountains
On an indoor horizon?
White lies, perhaps—the sort
Morality condones?
Or childish make-believe?

It's time the truth sank in—
That everything we see
With the eye is pure deception;
And that the particles
Which look like bee or orchid,
Mountain or foot, are islets
In a sea of emptiness;
Seen with the mind such lies
Are the one-and-only-truth.

PROMISED LAND

On every side flowers the promised land
    Calling me from this empty place; in a green
Sky the sunlit morning moon can stand
    Its ground against the sun and still be seen.

Rolling in play among the infant hills
    Are clouds of pearl, and far away as heaven
A wooded valley steeps and slowly fills
    From the end of the rainbow with a light not given

To any earthly nature. I take a pace
    In that direction, led by an icy hand:
But when I turn, I see the empty place
    Where I had stood become a promised land.

(Kenya, 1946)

IN ANDALUSIA

On the plains of Andalusia black cattle
    Nibble the wet grass, absorb the Spring;
At a glance you'd say they were a dairy herd,
    But look again: they are bulls bred for the ring.

They'll fight when taunted; with no inborn hatred
    Of man, and hampered by a low IQ,
They'll charge the red rag, not the matador
    Who waves it; can they guess what he will do

With that sharp sword? — No more aggressive than
    Ram, stallion, cock, these proud, pacific bulls
Exist for a fight, to be outclassed by man
    In a game of death,—and they don't fix the rules.

Equating virility with aggressiveness,
    Men flaunt their weakness: anger and disdain
For a grown bull which has no zest for fighting
    Reveal an infatuation with pain.

The healthy animal clings hard to life,
    But life-lovers don't stand a chance when faced
With matadors who brand them impotent,
    Flying red rags of derision and distaste.

On the hills of Andalusia, in the cities
    Stand Moorish palaces that remember how
Allah and Christ, for a spell, could breathe in peace,
    Neither goaded to lay the other low;

Trade flourished, poets sang, philosophers
    Scratched for the truth, and subtle artists carved
Shapes rivalling, not copying, Nature; who
    In that charmed hour was burned alive or starved?

It could not last: spokesmen of deities who
    Were not on speaking terms set fire to Spain;
In God's name tortured saints and thinkers: they
    Could find peace only through the gates of pain.

But then arose the Scapegoat, the black bull
    To lift a nation's guilt, typecast as wild,
Untameable, proud, though on these fertile plains
    As trusting and ingenuous as a child.

TWO RESURRECTIONS

(1) *Mayflower II,* 1957

Taking her motion from the sky,
   This Mayflower, like a phantom ship
Haunting a foreign century,
   Goes westward on her maiden trip.
Her photo, which at first sight looks
   Like some old print, at second sight
Fits in with poltergeists and spooks
   That hover between day and night.

No broken record can surprise
   A populace too bored to look
When someone flies up there at twice
   The speed of sound; but the earth shook
This morning, and the sky grew dark
   Under no thermonuclear test,
But in the shadow of this Ark
   Which sails once more to find the West.

(2) *Shakespeare's Globe*, 1995 (For Liza Vaughan-Hughes)

September dazzle... The born-again Globe
Welcomes its actors and its audience
Who cross a bridge (red carpet) from the work-day
London to this celebration. The Programme
Sings out the arrivals... 'Entry of the Poets'
(That means Heath-Stubbs and Enright and myself);
'Arrival of boys from Brambletye, for the picnic';
'Enter the Audience'... under a cobalt sky
Cluster the hatless groundlings; take their seats
In the covered outer circle the upper crust;
'Musicians strike up'... then the cascade
Of verse from where we fancy Shakespeare stood.
Boys, teachers, poets, one by one, stand up

To spout their lines,—mine hailing the Bard
On his four hundredth birthday.
                              But suddenly
A cold shiver … I seem to have bridged the years,
Four hundred of them, and this 'wooden "O" '
Is not a replica, but the original!
Those groundlings are not schoolboys and their parents,
But Bankside families of 1595;
And stranger still,—Heath-Stubbs and Enright
And I are Elizabethans, mouthing iambic
Greetings to our honoured neighbour, Will.
Who said the reversal of time-flow is impossible?
It happens every night in dreams—and dreams
May have more life to them than waking time!
So it didn't seem absurd when time-capsules
Full of our verses, neatly copied out
On parchment, signed quite legibly (for poets),
Were lowered and interred under the playhouse,
An offering to Time from a timeless place;
And did my roving eyebeams not catch sight,
As the capsules were being closed, of one
Containing a sonnet, all but illegible,
Signed with Renaissance flourish, 'William Shakespeare'?

FOR A FRIEND ON HIS
EIGHTIETH BIRTHDAY

'Never be ninety,' sighed old Wilfrid Meynell,
   Ninety himself. But eighty is not too bad:
Hardy was writing *Winter Words* and Verdi
   At work on *Falstaff* when he reached that age;

And Toscanini, eighty-five, conducted
   All the four symphonies of Brahms. 'Quite mad,'
His doctor may have thought, but Toscanini
   Knew them by heart, needed no printed page.

Eighty myself, I think this thought should please:
   Reaching that age unscathed, I'd say we're blest;
But even ninety suited Sophocles
   Who uttered, in his second *Oedipus*,
That paradox, 'Never to have lived is best'.
   Who knows, even ninety may prove good for us!

THE HEJNAL (For Krystyna Nazar)

Cracow, St. Mary's Church: from the high tower
   As the clock strikes twelve
      A trumpeter sounds the *Hejnal*—an alarm
Sounded in earnest when some foreign power
Threatened the city. Once, when Tartars came,
   A marksman shot the trumpeter
      Who fell, leaving the panic-tune unfinished;
Since when, to give the event its proper fame,
The fanfare is shot down in mid-flight
   Each day, as the hour strikes,
      The unfinished call blown to the four winds,
The trumpet but no trumpeter in sight;
A tiny sound is heard by gaping tourists
   In the Square—the horns of Elfland,
      A ghost-voice risen from the dead, which can't
Be exorcised by priests or scientists.
Through centuries such hauntings kept in sight
   Grievances best forgotten,
      Now relished, like the scars of battle wounds
Old soldiers show, as proof they once could fight.

Some day, for a lark, another trumpeter
   Will add the missing notes
      From a neighbouring roof. 'What's that? What's
                        going on?'
People will cry; in the turmoil, the great stir,
They'll hear a shout, 'Let the poor ghost have peace!
   Seven centuries are too long
      Even for a ghost to keep on haunting us.'
But then, with batons flashing, the police
Will put up roadblocks, hunt from door to door
   Until they trap the joker,
      Impound the offending instrument, and let

The *Hejnal* flourish as it did before—
Always unfinished, like a sun half set
  On the horizon, never
    Setting; never allowing the tired wound
To heal; ensuring no one shall forget.

ON THE LATE MASSACRE
IN LEBANON

Forget not; in thy book record their groans
Milton

And Death shall have no dominion
Dylan Thomas

'And Death' (note the initial ampersand,
   Meaning the words break in upon my thoughts)
'Shall have no dominion'... On the other hand
   Death is the cross on a battlefield of noughts,
The 'plus' that argues you were once alive;
   Death is your one-and-only destination—
Whether it is a pool in which you dive
   To emerge and find your permanent vocation,
Or simply the dead-end of your personal course.
   Today such thoughts don't comfort, are at best
A harsh irrelevance. My grief can't force
   One soul to return from the Islands of the Blest;
At least they are spared the holocaust to come:
There's an ounce of comfort in that thought for some.

A SECOND COMING (For Joe Hunt)

A second coming—late September roses
    Erupting while the garden goes to seed;
They revive a kind of hope, as when old men
    Notice there are sensations they still need—

The touch of a hand, the smile of a loved face;
    The kiss on meeting or on parting; shared
    Annoyance when plans founder, but when things
Work out as planned, shared joy, a warm embrace.

What right had we to expect more than that first
    Coming-of-age when, childish things put by,
We were suddenly plagued by a compelling thirst
    For strange sensations, for the discovery

Of a living god inside our bone and brain?
    That god fell short of immortality—
    The summer lost its grip, roses cracked up,
Yet now that rose tree comes to life again—

When I'm all set to laugh the whole thing off,
    To drown my book, bury my staff. I'll keep
    Those instruments of magic, and once more
Hold up the sun until I've had enough

Of daylight... When the magic fails, I'll beard
    That second, very different coming-of-Age
My spells won't exorcise; there must be a charm
    That works! It's not yet time to turn the page.

WINTER LANDSCAPE

Bristling with ash, crisp with elm and oak
　The hide of Nature can endure the lash
Of winter; can allow the world to soak
　And snore at ease, though gale and blizzard thrash
The tousled wood and whistle over the hill;
　Can go on sleeping when the angry furrows
Are smoothed and air grows luminous and still,
　Healing a hundred villages and boroughs.
But now a flame has caught the darkening air
　And fills the whole of space from heaven to earth,
Save for an oval window here and there—
　A glimpse of what we knew before our birth,
Cold and blue and unchanging, like the eye
Which keeps its light, whatever else may die.

PLACE AND TIME

Dying to go back
　To the places you like best,
You seek them out, arrive,
　And you are unimpressed.

But what you are really trying
　To do is to go back
　　To the *times* when you were happiest,
And doing that means dying.

ON HENGISTBURY HEAD, 1940

I've sent my herald thoughts ahead
  And follow at a speed, breaking the neck
Of Hengistbury Head.
  On that enormous brow a speck,
An ant, I follow the parting
  Until it peters out; then course
Through tangled yellow hair, smarting
  At knee and wrist from nettle and gorse.

I breathe the blue, exulting, and throw
  A stone a stone's throw toward
The sneering sea; blow
  A mocking kiss to the drunken horde
Of waves which, for a million years,
  Have roared and seethed in vain
To reach these cliffs; they prime our ears
  In patience, teach us to take pain.

Behind me sleeps the wished-for land;
  After the rain the streams, swollen,
Blue in the face and fanned
  By freezing north winds roll in
Obedient ranks, recruits for the sea…
  Over me three gulls look on,
Motionless, crossbows, — one of the three
  A quarter moon, its arrow gone.

A BONUS

Unique visibility:
In such clean air
The buildings, hills, trees show intimate detail
And seem, in a way,
To share the air's transparency.
Windows across the channel catch the sun,
Half-blinding me.
In the blue indoor light
Of corridors I seem to glide weightless,
Hardly touching the floor;
I catch translated looks on plain faces
And suddenly, for a sun-infused moment,
Wake to the fact
That life is a bonus; that war,
Famine, or some new plague
Resistant to every drug
Is bound eventually
To stub us out
Suddenly, or by stages.
So cherish these infusions
Of open sky, moments
Of ecstatic unconcern; even
Welcome a wild
Apocalyptic
Exit.

EXIT TIME

Each particle of life, each book he read,
Each journey that he made seemed to exist
In order that he might remember it,
Not as a sketch, an item in some list,
But in full colour, in all four dimensions:
He even lost some of the instant pleasure
In fears about what details he'd forget.

But age has sheared away the dense coat
Of memories that screened him from the cold:
Dreaded amnesia... Strangely, though, he feels
Comfort he never knew till he was old,
Happy to remember hardly anything;
Lives in the moment. Pleasures long forgotten
He relishes once more—for the first time!

No longer chained to the possessive past
And the uncertain future, every moment
Seems more complete and every joy more perfect,
Set free at last from the corrosive torment
Of memory. Time seems to have stopped going,
Though, strangely, something different fills his field
Of vision every time he looks around.

VISITING CARDS

My mother's euphemism for mouse droppings in the larder:
how apt it seems now as I spring-clean a drawer
and find, among thirty years' junk, this heap of visiting
    cards!
The names on most are forgotten; some are stiff; some
    jocular
('John and Jenny Geburtstag, Philadelphia, Consulting
    Grandparents':
with 'We R Retired' in gothic script on the back of the card).
Some names reverberate without calling to mind
face or fortune. A few should not have come to light—
this one, for instance: seeing the name rejuvenates my
    world
for a moment: I hear the gay parting shots, the shouts of
'till next year'... 'till the summer...' our toasts and
    promises
ring down three decades: now he's dead or, at best, a
    stranger:
we'd pass each other in the street without recognition.
And only this morning a visitor from Japan pressed a card
upon me as we said good-bye... I waited for him to go,
then hurriedly threw his card into the waste-paper basket.

THE DOLL

"She is older than I am,"
Chuckles the old woman,
Pointing a shrivelled finger
At the child propped in a pram
Bolt-upright, blinking
When budged, its chubby face
Smooth and expressionless—
The doll she had for Christmas
Ninety years ago.
Unearthed from a dark cupboard,
A toy which was too big
For her, but did not grow,
Now comes into its own.
"It was so tall," she muses,
"So much like me, people
Mistook it for my twin."
And now, bridging the gap
Of ninety years, she sees
A twin's eyes look back;
Slowly forgets the map
Of rivulets and wrinkles
Through which she talks to us—
And the doll seems to smile
Back from a looking-glass.

COUNT-DOWN

A new discovery: I have started hearing
   My own pulse. It sounds
Like the deep breathing of another body,
   Not part of me. I hear it
At night, in silent hours when there's no traffic
   To drown the beat. It wakes me up,
Keeps me awake. I swallow, breathe hard
   To stop it; turn my pillow, hold
My breath; nothing helps… but then it fades
   In its own time, of its own accord.

Is it the count-down for my take-off, heart
   Heralding its own arrest?
It scares me when I look at it that way,
   But I am galvanised
By the stranger in my bed, the heavy breathing
   Close to my inner ear,
The visitor with a will of its own. —How long
   Before it drops to 'zero'?
Unheard, that counting started long ago
   Before my birth, a silent song.

BATH TIME

It seems I am being purified,
Not merely washed clean
By the water of Time; this soothing warmth
Smoothes the furrows of anxiety
Across my brow, and seems to erase
The wrinkles of old age,
The dust of ages, the guilt
Of anger—till suddenly I find
The ruins of my infancy restored,
And once again I seem
To be that thoughtless innocent
Caged in his earthly paradise.
But Time, now flowing backwards,
Washes away necessities that seem
To have become impurities;
Is washing most of me away—
And now it is carrying me back,
While I still enjoy the light,
To Mother Earth's dark and oblivious womb.

MYSTIC BRIDGE*

On the expressway, where the roads divide,
  A sign, MYSTIC BRIDGE,
    Stuns the eye. Suddenly,
As though I had shaken off an official guide
And come, by chance, on the alternative route
  Hidden since infancy,
    I seem to step across
To the lost paradise—a first foot
Into a year of sunflowers. Strange, that a word
  Should have such influence,
    Brushing my workday thoughts aside
And making sense of what might seem absurd,
A second chance, a backward pilgrimage
  From our disjointed scene
    To the harmony of an earlier day—
And approachable only across the Mystic Bridge.

* A bridge across the Mystic River, Boston, Massachusetts